CONTENTS

1)	Introduction to F. Scott Fitzgerald	1
2)	Textual Analysis	
	Book I	25
	Book II	34
3)	Character Analyses	39
4)	Essay Questions and Answers	41
5)	Critical Commentary	45
6)	Essay Questions and Answers	58
7)	Critical Review	62
8)	Bibliography	69

BRIGHT NOTES

TENDER IS THE NIGHT AND THIS SIDE OF PARADISE BY F. SCOTT FITZGERALD

Intelligent Education

Nashville, Tennessee

BRIGHT NOTES: Tender Is the Night and This Side of Paradise
www.BrightNotes.com

No part of this publication may be used or reproduced in any manner whatsoever without written permission, except in the case of brief quotations in critical articles and reviews. For permissions, contact Influence Publishers http://www.influencepublishers.com.

ISBN: 978-1-645421-26-9 (Paperback)
ISBN: 978-1-645421-27-6 (eBook)

Published in accordance with the U.S. Copyright Office Orphan Works and Mass Digitization report of the register of copyrights, June 2015.

Originally published by Monarch Press.
Stanley Cooperman, 1965
2020 Edition published by Influence Publishers.

Interior design by Lapiz Digital Services. Cover Design by Thinkpen Designs.

Printed in the United States of America.

Library of Congress Cataloging-in-Publication Data forthcoming.
Names: Intelligent Education
Title: BRIGHT NOTES: Tender Is the Night and This Side of Paradise
Subject: STU004000 STUDY AIDS / Book Notes

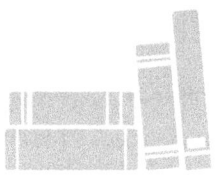

INTRODUCTION TO F. SCOTT FITZGERALD

"Rich people," said Ernest Hemingway, "are poor people with money." It seemed to F. Scott Fitzgerald, however, that they were nothing of the sort, and he devoted a good part of his work to proving that "rich people" are indeed "different from you and me."

That Hemingway insisted upon reducing a complexity to some sort of manageable simplicity was totally characteristic of him both as a person and as a writer. And that Fitzgerald knew, perhaps all too well, that money was a crucial element in American culture, shaped the successes and failures of his work - and of his life.

THE 'CITY BOY'

Like Ernest Hemingway, Francis Scott Key Fitzgerald was born in "the provinces" of America: the Midwest. Unlike Hemingway, however (who was profoundly influenced by the great outdoors so much a part of his small-town childhood), Fitzgerald was born in a large city - St. Paul, Minnesota - and remained a "city boy" all his life. His family, moreover, was very much a part of St. Paul "society," and this too had considerable influence in determining the direction of his art, and the growth of his sensibility.

Perhaps one might say that it was simply a matter of a different sort of wilderness, but one thing is clear: if many of Hemingway's basic attitudes were shaped by his experiences hunting and fishing in the great North woods, many of Fitzgerald's basic attitudes were defined by the upper middle-class financial and social position that was his heritage.

Fitzgerald's maternal grandfather was the St. Paul merchant P. F. McQuillan, a hard-working man with the integrity and "soundness" so characteristic of the middle-merchant group of the area. Although the McQuillan fortune by no means belonged to the foremost rank of St. Paul money, the wholesale grocery business founded by the old man was worth over a million dollars at his death, and the McQuillan will left $250,000 to be shared by Fitzgerald's mother and the four other McQuillan children: two sisters and two brothers. That the McQuillan name was one of "substance" in St. Paul is indicated by the fact that Fitzgerald's own activities at Princeton, where he achieved a modest success as both a playwright and athlete, received considerable coverage in the society pages of St. Paul newspapers.

FITZGERALD'S 'SOCIETY' BACKGROUND

It was primarily due to his mother's family that Fitzgerald could be described as someone "born into the country club set." The family's position in this set, however, was rather ambiguous; neither "aristocrats" nor "nobodies," they dwelt in a kind of social twilight zone best symbolized by Fitzgerald's own description of one of the houses in which he lived as a St. Paul teenager: it was, he says, "a house below the average on a street above the average."

Such a position is hardly conducive to personal security, and perhaps helps explain why F. Scott Fitzgerald, while born into the exclusive "club" of the privileged class, spent a lifetime worrying about his membership - and worrying, too, whether the membership itself was worth the emotional and artistic energy he felt obliged (often in spite of his own better judgment) to expend in order to maintain it.

On his mother's side, at any rate, Fitzgerald was the inheritor of a tradition in which financial "success" was still defined by a strong awareness of moral solidity, an ethical responsibility, a tradition in which "good" business was directly related rather than irrelevant to good citizenship and social responsibility. It was, indeed, the kind of firmly based ethic referred to by Nick Carroway, narrator of Fitzgerald's finest work- *The Great Gatsby*- as he wishes for a world that would "stand at moral attention forever."

And the nostalgia for such a world was, certainly, to become an important aspect of F. Scott Fitzgerald's rather schizophrenic personal development.

A MORAL PROVINCIAL

Under the veneer of Princetonian aestheticism and despite his need for a "smart" identity (to be earned by "success"), Fitzgerald, in a very profound sense, remained a moral provincial; and it is precisely this moral "provincialism" - the nostalgia for moral qualities represented by the West and the scorn of the moral vacuum represented by the "East" - which is so basic to the dramatic structure of *The Great Gatsby*.

Throughout Fitzgerald's work, indeed, there is a tension between the pursuit of wealth (or an acknowledgment of the power of wealth), and a distrust of the wealth itself when it lacks the support of moral responsibility, and so becomes merely an instrument for the gratification of impulse. As such an instrument, wealth becomes destructive, and the American Dream-which is based on wealth-turns into the American Nightmare, the "Fitzgerald Woman" - with her charm, her parasitism, and her fatal lack of allegiance to anything but sentimental impulse (the gratification of which is made possible by wealth) - emerges as kind of child-Princess of doom, a "Golden Girl" whose very beauty becomes a form of vampirism.

The "solid" tradition of the McQuillans, however, was not part of the background of Fitzgerald's father-or rather, the tradition was of a different sort, at once more "romantic" and more vaguely defined. For Edward Fitzgerald's Maryland family could - and did - trace its kinship back to Francis Scott Key; and Edward Fitzgerald was himself something of a Southern gentleman whose manners were far more impressive than was his business acumen. Neither as a corporation executive nor as a broker was he particularly successful, and Fitzgerald's father remains a shadowy figure in the author's life.

Shortly after Fitzgerald's birth, on September 24, 1896, the family moved to Buffalo, New York, and lived for a time in Syracuse. After Edward Fitzgerald lost his job with Procter and Gamble, however, the family returned to St. Paul, and it was in St. Paul that Scott reached his adolescence. By this time both his parents were past fifty. His father seemed to become more "Southern" as it became increasingly obvious that his business career had reached a dead end, and his mother, having lost two previous children, lavished a rather baroque devotion on young Scott. The development of Scott as a "mamma's boy" was to shape many of his attitudes as an adult-a fact noted by many commentators on Fitzgerald's life and work.

The only other Fitzgerald child to survive childbirth was a girl, Annabel, but it was Scott who remained the focus of his parents' attention. Although details of Fitzgerald's early years in upstate New York are rather sketchy, the final portrait, as Kenneth Eble remarks, is that of "a somewhat pampered and sheltered boy, an occupant of apartments and rented houses, an inheritor of a sense of family superiority without much visible means to support it."

EARLY ADOLESCENCE

Back in St. Paul, the young Fitzgerald attended St. Paul Academy, where he demonstrated a growing affinity for literature. He published a short story in the school magazine, and kept copious journals. Even as an adolescent, however, Scott's attitude toward literature was ambiguous; writing, indeed, seems to have been merely one method among many for securing social status and "leadership," and Scott devoted himself with no less enthusiasm to club politics and athletics, not to mention "dancing class," as a means of achieving the status he so intensely craved even as a boy.

Reviewing his later career at Princeton, commentators have often wondered whether Fitzgerald's literary career would ever have come into existence had he been more physically suited for a major athletic career, or more emotionally suited for a sustained effort at campus politics. There is considerable justice, certainly, in the charge that for F. Scott Fitzgerald literature was a means rather than an end. Even as a schoolboy he felt no particular sense of vocation in literature, and his later career was to be seriously hampered by the fact that, for various reasons, Fitzgerald was forced to use his work as a key to open doors which otherwise would have remained closed, at least for him.

Such argument, of course, can easily be overstated; one can no more define the actual literature produced by Fitzgerald according to his motives in producing it, than one can define the prose rhythms of a writer like James Joyce through a mere description of his poor eyesight. What Edmund Wilson calls the "Sacred Wound" of the artist simply does not define the essence- or the value-of the art itself; and if the "Sacred Wound" of F. Scott Fitzgerald was a chronic inability to do his work for the sake of the work itself, one might also note that in this respect, as in so many others, his own conflicts represented the conflicts of his time and his culture.

In art, perhaps more than in any other field of human endeavor, personal weakness is no less a resource than is personal strength; the artist, indeed, very often uses his work to redeem the weakness itself-weakness which becomes, in a basic sense, a raw material of the art. It is true, for example, that if Ernest Hemingway had possessed greater social sensitivity and objective intelligence, his work would have been richer; but it is also true that the unique power of his work depended, to a great extent, on the lack of certain qualities which in themselves and in general terms are quite desirable. It would be foolish, after all, to attack Hemingway because he was not Henry James.

FITZGERALD AND LITERARY 'PURITY'

By the same token, to accuse Fitzgerald of having lacked certain elements of literary purity found in other writers, is actually to make a retrospective demand that he ought to have been somebody else. That he was not somebody else, is a fact for which readers ought to be thankful. Granted that Fitzgerald's weaknesses prevented his development along certain lines, they also created his development along others, and this is also true of writers like Hemingway, or Faulkner, or any other individual who sets himself the task of working words into literature. Given Fitzgerald's personal and social insecurities, one must indeed admit that he could never have written *A Farewell to Arms*. And given Hemingway's own fears and preoccupations, he could not have produced books like *This Side of Paradise* or *Tender is the Night*, let alone a novel with the unique value of *The Great Gatsby*.

It is possible, in short, to recognize that Fitzgerald's preoccupation with social status and "making good" took up much of his energy throughout his career, while also recognizing that the value of his best work is the result of precisely this preoccupation. And if there were certain qualities of adolescence and romance which Fitzgerald in his own way (like Hemingway in his) never outgrew, it was these qualities which provided the raw material for those Fitzgerald works which remain a vital contribution to American literature.

In 1911, Fitzgerald entered a Catholic boarding school in Hackensack, New Jersey-the Newman Academy, at which he spent two years. During this time he visited New York on several occasions, saw several plays, and continued his own apprenticeship in literature. He wrote several dramas, one of which was produced at school with Fitzgerald himself playing the lead: that of a very sophisticated "gentleman" burglar. And it was also during this time that Fitzgerald became aware of the glowing, romantic, and-for him-destructive power of sex, a power idealized into melodramatic sentiment, darkened by adolescent "disillusions," and surrounded by fears and distractions which he never completely outgrew.

THE FIRST ROMANCE

It was Ginerva King, a wealthy Chicago girl, who shaped his desire for - and fear of - the sort of "enchanting," careless, and essentially superficial female who was to reappear so often in his stories and novels: women like Rosalind in *This Side of Paradise*, or Gloria in *Tender is the Night*, or Daisy in *The Great Gatsby*-women who, despite their physical charm, are characterized by a profound emotional frigidity based partially upon a need for romantic posture, and partially upon a sort of instinctive calculation which leads them to use and exploit, and-when necessary-to discard their men rather than love them completely.

Fitzgerald actually met Ginerva after he had already entered Princeton; it was during Christmas vacation of 1915 that he began his "romance." The intensity of his emotion, however, was a source of embarrassment rather than joy for the young lady, who stopped answering his letters and ultimately married another man. Fitzgerald, deeply hurt, retreated into himself, and-as he so often did in times of adversity-retreated back to St. Paul as well.

A PERIOD OF DEFEAT

The next few years of Fitzgerald's life was a period of personal defeat and continued chaos. Forced to withdraw from Princeton because of the sordid matter of low grades, he spent nine rather aimless months at home, and returned to Princeton in 1916 trailing the rags and tatters of his various campus ambitions behind him.

The Princeton experience, together with the half-absurd bitterness of his relations with Ginerva King, his own background of semi-wealth, and his awareness both of the world of privilege represented by wealth and the changes wrought in that world by the impact of World War I (the moral and ethical loss of direction resulting from the impact itself), was to be rather lushly recreated in *This Side of Paradise*.

AUTOBIOGRAPHICAL MATERIAL

Autobiographical material, of course, was to be a vital element in the work of F. Scott Fitzgerald. Both his novels and stories-even such comparatively objective works such as *The Great Gatsby* or *Tender is the Night*-deal with his own experiences, or rather use such experiences as a focus for defining the enormous moral changes occurring in the United States.

Unlike many other writers of the twenties, who either "retreated" from America after the war, or attempted to objectify it through a broad-scope sociological analysis, or ridiculed it through **parody**, F. Scott Fitzgerald saw in himself precisely those aspects of "The American Dream" which had caused its own degradation. And for this reason the element of autobiography in his work is aesthetically and culturally valuable. "One of the most remarkable things about Scott Fitzgerald as a writer," remarks the critic Arthur Mizener in *Afternoon of an Author*, "is the dual character of his self-knowledge . . . ":

The curious way in which he combined the innocence of complete involvement with an almost scientific coolness and observation, so that he nearly always wrote about deeply felt personal experience, and nearly always as if the important use of personal experience was to illustrate general truths.

So, too, the critic Alfred Kazin, in *F. Scott Fitzgerald*, comments on Fitzgerald's work:

[It] is full of precisely observed external detail, for which he had a formidable memory, and it is the gift of observation which has led to the opinion that he was nothing but a chronicler of social surface, particularly of the twenties. Yet, for all its concrete external detail, his work is very personal. The events of his stories are nearly always events in which Fitzgerald has himself participated with all his emotional energy.

F. Scott Fitzgerald, in short, did not "retreat" from America (either into art-for-art's sake, or the bull ring), and neither did he attempt any grandiose rendering of national culture. Using what he knew-what he himself had, either directly or vicariously, experienced before the war or in postwar America-Fitzgerald dramatized the dreams, and the illusions, which he felt to be at the core of America's greatness - and loss of greatness.

Like the Irish novelist James Joyce, who pledged himself to "forge, in the smithy of my soul, the uncreated conscience of my race," Fitzgerald focused upon personal experience which was indeed a microcosm of the experience of his nation. And in this sense, the work of Fitzgerald-while obviously "autobiographical" - transcends the personal, and becomes a dramatic symbol of human and cultural reality. His experiences at Princeton, his experiences with the fatal and parasitic "golden girl" who was to reappear so often in his books and who was to exercise so profound an effect on his life, his awareness of violently changing moral codes (which he was to regard with a mixture of fascination and repugnance) - these were vitally part of the development of American culture no less than they were part of the development of Fitzgerald as a writer and as a man.

THE PROBLEM OF WEALTH

Scott's preoccupation with the problems of wealth for example- with the central importance of money, and the dreams, the magical expectations, the carelessness," the ideals and the illusions which both create and are created by wealth - was certainly a very personal matter for him as an individual. As critic Malcolm Cowley remarked: Fitzgerald was like "a little boy pressing his face against a window, looking at a party to which he was not invited, and wondering who was paying the bills."

But this adolescent sense of exclusion, the vision of life as a "party" at which perpetually glowing men and girls achieved happiness-by-invitation, was essential to that adolescent Romance which Fitzgerald perceived to be at the very core of American "materialism," a uniquely romantic materialism which itself was the paradox, and the pathos, of American cultural development.

Fitzgerald's return to Princeton, at any rate, was short-lived; when he took up his academic pursuits for the fall term in 1917, Scott (like so many other young college men) was both distracted and delighted at the excitement of the European war, now America's war as well. His school career came to an end when he was inducted into the army, and the prospect of military adventure-together with his engagement to Zelda Sayre, a lovely Alabama girl of good family with a background of considerable wealth-seemed to offer some alternative to the emotional and intellectual drifting, the profound futility caused by his earlier failure at the university and by his previous relationship with Ginerva King.

ZELDA: FITZGERALD'S 'GOLDEN GIRL'

Both his hopes for military adventure and his hopes for a Supreme Love, however, seemed to collapse in rather ludicrous fashion: the war ended before Fitzgerald had so much as caught a glimpse of action (indeed, he never left the country), and his engagement to Zelda foundered in a welter of rejection slips. For after being discharged from the army in 1919, Fitzgerald had set about "earning" his Golden Girl by trying to write fiction while holding down a ninety-dollar a month advertising job. The magazines rejected his stories, and Zelda rejected Fitzgerald. There was a brutal simplicity to Zelda's action that Fitzgerald never forgot, and indeed, it provided a basic **theme** of his work: the **theme** of the delicate, lovely, and essentially parasitic woman whose affections - and loyalty - had to be "acquired" by success and protected by continued success, so that love itself, like a kind of stock-dividend, depended upon perpetual "investment" of emotional funds that were always threatening to be depleted.

Zelda herself, indeed, appears in many of Fitzgerald's works: in *The Great Gatsby*, she becomes Daisy Buchanan, whose voice "is full of money"; in *Tender is the Night*, she becomes the parasitic Nicole, first using and then discarding Dick Diver; even in *This Side of Paradise* such women as Rosalind or Beatrice Blaine (mother of the **protagonist**, Amory Blaine) prefigure the lovely but parasitic figures who are so fascinating and so deadly to Fitzgerald and his characters.

That Scott never forgot the manner in which Zelda broke their engagement is obvious not merely from his use of the

episode in his fiction, but also from his comments in various journals and memoirs and letters. In one of these journals, for example, he vividly describes the "lesson" he learned from Zelda:

The man with a jingle of money in his pocket who married the girl a year later would always cherish an abiding distrust, an animosity toward the leisure class - not the conviction of a revolutionary, but the smoldering resentment of a peasant. In the years since then I have never stopped wondering where my friends' money came from, nor stopped thinking that at one time a sort of droit de seigneur might have been exercised to give one of them my girl.

The phrase droit de seigneur refers to the medieval custom by which the Lord of the Manor had the right to sample any bride about to be married within his domain; that Fitzgerald would use such a term to describe the woman he loved is itself an indication of how powerfully his imagination had been affected by the reality of money - and the fact that "Love," no matter how "Romantic," is very much a part of such reality.

Fitzgerald's comment is also very relevant to his work in that he makes a distinction between the "conviction of a revolutionary" and the "smoldering resentment of a peasant." For neither Fitzgerald nor his **protagonists** (not even Amory Blaine, despite his verbal gesture at radicalism which sets the tone for the rather pathetic conclusion of *This Side of Paradise*) really question the system itself. Awed by the power, the "magic" and careless grace of the wealthy, they do not challenge "the system" but rather occupy themselves with acquiring whatever baubles the system has to offer-baubles which indeed have a half-absurd and half-tragic importance because they become the only means of acquiring love, loyalty, and the chimera of imagined "happiness" - always "golden," always vaguely defined, always just beyond the locked fraternity door of some exclusive tomorrow.

After Zelda broke their engagement, at any rate, Fitzgerald quit his advertising job - and in his own word - "crept" back to St. Paul to finish a novel, hoping to earn literary fame, financial security, and a wife, all at the same time. And he did just that.

THE BIG-TIME

It was, of course, a remarkable "pay off." When Scribners accepted the manuscript of *This Side of Paradise* in 1919, life turned into a Irish sweepstakes, with Fitzgerald holding all the winning tickets. Suddenly the "breaks" were going his way, and the Great American Dream of "striking it rich" had, almost inexplicably, become a reality.

The big markets-*Smart Set*, *Saturday Evening Post*, and *Scribner's Magazine*-accepted a total of nine Fitzgerald stories as though on cue, and after *This Side of Paradise* appeared in 1920 to mixed critical notices but immediate popular success, Zelda picked up her cue as well: she and Fitzgerald were married in New York's St. Patrick's Cathedral. The world, for F. Scott Fitzgerald and his enchanting wife, was a fantasy come true, a party where champagne and kisses flowed like money, while the American reading public paid the bills.

It cannot be stressed too heavily that Fitzgerald's courtship of Zelda was in many ways the vital experience of his life. The matter was actually quite simple: either he proved that he was a "success" and won the girl, or he did not prove that he was a success, and lost the girl. Money, in short, was the magic wand that would turn the land of ashes into a Golden Palace, and Zelda was a Fairy Princess with a price tag attached to each gossamer wing.

Fitzgerald himself describes the intense money-consciousness that filled his mind after his discharge from the army. Even his novel was an "ace in the hole" to be used for a poker game in which Zelda represented the stakes. "I was in love with a whirlwind," said Fitzgerald, "and I must spin a net big enough to catch it out of my head, a head full of trickling nickels and sliding dimes, the incessant music-box of the poor."

But Fitzgerald did indeed catch "the whirlwind"; the golden boy of American literature (he was in his early twenties when *This Side of Paradise* appeared) married his golden girl, and the year he and Zelda spent in New York (from the spring of 1920 to the spring of 1921) was a true-life fulfillment of "the infinite promise of American advertising." It was, as Fitzgerald later put it, the start of a "carnival" which was to continue for several years in Europe as well as in New York, a merry-go-round which, at least for a time, featured an inexhaustible supply of golden rings.

Despite its popular success, *This Side of Paradise* was rather churlishly received by serious critics, who saw the book as the work of a brilliant but generally unfocused talent. The structure of the novel is, of course, loosely episodic; provided with a minimum of plot coherence by the education of its "central" **protagonist**, Amory Blaine, *This Side of Paradise* was, as Fitzgerald himself remarked in one of his letters, a "picaresque ramble," and as such lacked either narrative or intellectual point.

THIS SIDE OF PARADISE

The very lack of a solid intellectual or social position, however, was itself one reason why *This Side of Paradise* seemed to dramatize so well the postwar mood of romance and futility, expectation and disillusion, "rebellion" and inconsequence. Reviewing the book in 1922, for example, the critic Edmund Wilson (who was to become one of the most sensitive and perceptive of Fitzgerald commentators), remarked that "*This Side of Paradise* is not really about anything; intellectually it amounts to little more than a gesture - a gesture of indefinite revolt."

But it was the very "indefinite" quality of the revolt which made the book so appealing-the very naivete and lack of firm intellectual commitment even to rebellion captured a vital aspect of the postwar mood, a mood in which sex was often asserted without sensuality, radicalism embraced without ideology, and "success" worshipped without achievement.

Perhaps more important than the book's lack of intellectual substance was the fact that-as many critics were soon to remark- Fitzgerald himself lacked a certain objectivity in his presentation: he seemed, indeed, uncertain as to his own attitude toward his protagonists, and also seemed to assert precisely those values of romance and carelessness, of tinsel and moonlight, which sometimes, he attempted to mock.

The book, in short, seemed to be the work of a young man altogether too preoccupied with his own posture as writer, a young man whose imagination had been shaped by the vaporing's of prewar aestheticism, and rather precociously "smartened" by postwar revelations and "new freedoms." Even in this respect, however, Fitzgerald was profoundly representative of his generation, a generation which, after all, had been a "Victorian" generation indeed, and had embarked on the Great Crusade of World War I - and the Great Hangover which replaced the crusade - with a singular mixture of bitterness and enthusiasm: qualities which themselves had been based upon cultural and intellectual naivete.

MONEY, MONEY, MONEY

Critical doubts notwithstanding, at any rate, *This Side of Paradise* began an enchanted period in Fitzgerald's life; a male Cinderella, he had achieved his Golden Princess - Zelda - and the two young people enjoyed their dream-come-true. Along with the parties, however, there were bills. Fitzgerald was actually living a frenetic life at this time, accumulating debts despite the explosive increase of his income, and turning out stories as though his typewriter were a money-machine. In retrospect, it seems almost astonishing that he produced some of his best short fiction during this time, and completed his second novel as well-*The Beautiful and the Damned*, which appeared as a serial in 1921 (in *Metropolitan Magazine*), and was published in book form in 1922.

Fitzgerald was to describe this period of his career as "the greatest, gaudiest spree in history," but, if his work is any indication, he himself sensed a core of rottenness beneath the surface of the splendor: a basic theme of his work was the futility, or rather the exhausting and febrile rush to nowhere which somehow seemed to characterize even the brightest promise of "success."

After a brief and largely uneventful trip to Europe, Fitzgerald and Zelda returned to St. Paul, where their daughter Frances was born; they then returned to New York, entered another round of the Gay Life, and finally rented a house in Great Neck, Long

Island - an area which was to provide the setting for *The Great Gatsby*. Meanwhile the conflict between Fitzgerald's artistic hopes and need for money - and for providing all the baubles which Zelda demanded from life as a tribute to her existence-continued and intensified.

Zelda, said Fitzgerald later, "wanted me to work for her and not enough for my dream." It was not, however, that simple; the "dream" of F. Scott Fitzgerald, glittering with much false gold, was neither constantly nor clearly defined-even to himself.

THE GREAT GATSBY

In 1924, on the strength of a renewed production of stories and income, the Fitzgeralds went abroad once again, and this time the excursion was to last over two years. *The Great Gatsby* appeared in 1925, and although Fitzgerald himself felt that he had at last produced a truly important work ("My book is wonderful," he wrote to Edmund Wilson from France) the book received mixed notices from the reviewers, and-perhaps more important, at least in immediate terms-fell far short of the financial harvest produced by the two previous novels. Never again was Fitzgerald to strike it really "rich"; neither *Gatsby* nor *Tender is the Night* (his last completed novel, published in 1934) were best-sellers - an **irony**, of course, in the light of subsequent critical judgment.

But there was much justice to Fitzgerald's faith in *The Great Gatsby*, a novella of great symbolic richness and narrative economy, a morality tale of Idealism rendered pathetic and ultimately destroyed by a world in which Idealism itself is corrupted into random appetite and demands of materialism, while the face of "God" is advertised on billboards.

The Great Gatsby is not (and was not intended to be) a documentary study of social complexities or social abuses. The book is rather a lyrical rendering of a perception into American values based upon what Fitzgerald understood to be the central paradox of his own "biography" and the biography of his nation: a uniquely romantic "materialism" in which men attempt to create a glowing Ideal from material acquisition; in which - with no less "faith" than that necessary for any other mystic rite - they attempt to convince themselves that desire can define reality, that gesture can define action, and that sentiment can define emotion.

There is, in short, at the heart of *The Great Gatsby* - and of American materialism itself - a peculiar innocence, what Andrew Turnbull calls "the extraordinary gift for hope and romantic readiness," symbolized by Jay Gatsby as he builds his "enchanted palace" for Daisy Buchanan. And Daisy in turn represents what Nick Carroway, narrator of the book, terms "a vast, vulgar, meretricious beauty." It is the non-material or ideal quality of this materialism which makes of Jay Gatsby a perpetual innocent, a dreaming adolescent, a uniquely American Don Quixote tilting at windmills with a lance of gold, winning his Enchanted Princess, and counting his silk shirts as though they were rosaries. And there was, of course, much of Fitzgerald himself in both Gatsby and Nick, the latter expressing an affirmation (or perhaps one should say a nostalgia) for the traditional moral codes of the Midwest.

THE WALTZ SLOWS DOWN

Meanwhile, Fitzgerald's drinking had become both more intense and less "fun" than it ever had been. Long "rows" with Zelda ended in passionate reconciliations well-lubricated with tears and with alcohol, and while Zelda moved inexorably toward her mental breakdown, pursuing her own fantasies of a "career" in ballet and as a writer in her own right, Fitzgerald moved closer to the bottle.

Most of the years between 1924 and 1931 were spent abroad, and it was during this time that Fitzgerald became an intimate friend of Ernest Hemingway. At the beginning of their relationship, indeed, it was Fitzgerald who was the "established" writer and Hemingway who was the unknown; by the end of the decade, however, their roles were reversed, with Hemingway well on his way to a career as "The Champ," and Fitzgerald the "has been" writer whom Hemingway was to characterize so sharply in his story "The Snows of Kilimanjaro."

BOTTLES AND BREAKDOWNS

Much of the Fitzgeralds' time during these years was spent on the Riviera, although they moved across Europe from Paris to the sea with a restlessness which itself was born of despair rather than happiness. Zelda became more unbalanced, had one breakdown in Switzerland, and devoted herself to a short-lived career as a ballerina, while Fitzgerald found it increasingly difficult to work; a man hardly into his thirties, he was convinced that his career was all but finished. They returned to America in 1931. Zelda's father died shortly afterward, and Zelda had her second breakdown in 1932.

Living in Baltimore, while recuperating from her second attack, Zelda began *Save Me the Waltz* - an autobiographical novel which represented, she said, an attempt at a sort of self-therapy through work. Fitzgerald, however, saw the book in a somewhat different light. Zelda's motives, he wrote, were to reduce her husband to a "non-entity," to cut him down as a man of literature as she already had, in so many ways, cut down his manhood itself (and in this connection readers of Fitzgerald will find much fascinating material in Hemingway's posthumous *A Moveable Feast*).

While Zelda's condition worsened, Fitzgerald himself reacted to the shambles of his personal life by increasingly heavy drinking. He continued to work, however, and although his income had all but vanished, an important product of this period was *Tender is the Night*, written between bouts of illness, alcoholism, and all too obvious evidence that the condition of Zelda was becoming hopeless. After an attempted suicide, Zelda suffered her final breakdown in 1934, and entered the clinic at Johns Hopkins University. She was to spend the rest of her life in various sanitariums.

TENDER IS THE NIGHT

In many ways *Tender is the Night* is a recapitulation of **themes** already explored in *The Great Gatsby*: once again there is the "Fitzgerald female" (this time drawn along lines for which Zelda's illness provided much of the raw material), first using and then turning away from an essentially romantic hero ruined by his own idealism. Once again there is the "world of the rich" - a careless, ruthless world, the masters of which (like Tom Buchanan in *Gatsby*) are able to survive precisely because of their lack of sentiment. And once again there is the all-important **theme** of money, always so vital a force in Fitzgerald's imagination, and always closely allied with love and with sex itself. "Money," remarks the critic D. S. Savage, "here would appear in some obscure way to be the agent of feminine sexuality; by its means Dick, robbed of his male potency-the historical will to vocation, work, culture-has fallen into subjection to the natural female will to idleness and pleasure."

It is less, however, the "female will" that ultimately ruins Dick Diver, than it is the indulgence of impulse, a kind of "need" characterized by the lack of any will at all. Nicole, indeed, the "patient" whom Dick marries (and who exploits whatever strength he has to offer before turning, like Daisy Buchanan, to the brutal force and direction of an assertive lover), is morally incomplete because she herself feeds on the will of her man; ironically, it is precisely this flaw which finally insures her survival and "cure" in a world where moral will is a guarantee not of survival, but of destruction.

Dick, then, is ruined not despite his goodness, but because of it; in the moral wasteland those who give (rather than take) are simply drained and tossed aside, while morality itself, or the pursuit of ideal value, is associated with both weakness and impotence. Like Ed Wilson, who in *The Great Gatsby* makes the fatal error of actually loving; and like Gatsby, who commits the no less fatal error of devoting himself to an Ideal, Dick Diver in *Tender is the Night* makes the mistake of first rescuing and then loving a Fairy Princess of Money. The result is inevitable: he is, quite simply, consumed.

Tender is the Night received mixed critical notices in 1934, and although Fitzgerald remained the subject of some perceptive literary comment, he seemed to be a "dated" literary figure, of interest largely to a limited circle of those who had known him personally. After 1935 his work was thin, although the essays later edited by Edmund Wilson as part of *The Crack-Up* (which appeared in 1945) continue to be of great interest, especially with the resurgence of Fitzgerald's reputation in the last two decades.

THE END OF A SAGA

Despite an inheritance from his mother's death in 1936, Fitzgerald was deeply in debt, and worked in Hollywood partly in order to pay off his creditors. Illness, alcohol, and personal instability marked his last years; except for a continued close relationship with his daughter, and a rather poignant attraction to Sheila Graham, he seemed incapable of any sustained social contact.

In 1939 Fitzgerald began work on a new novel, *The Last Tycoon*, which he never completed. Although the fragment was extravagantly praised on its first appearance, critical judgment has tended to reinforce the impression that the continued emotional and physical exhaustion of Fitzgerald's life had taken its toll: *The Last Tycoon*-described by Fitzgerald himself as "an escape into a lavish, romantic past that will not come again in our time" - is something of an echo of the Gatsby **theme** (the "Dream" doomed by its own terms), but without the vital cultural relevance and narrative economy which make *The Great Gatsby* a major work of American literature, and without the retrospective control, the objectivity, which shaped *Tender is the Night*.

In 1940 the second of two heart attacks killed F. Scott Fitzgerald. Seven years later, Zelda Fitzgerald burned to death in a sanitarium. The saga of the Fitzgeralds had come to an end. The "failure" of Scott Fitzgerald, however, in all its pathos, its vitality, and its brilliance, had been the sort of "failure" that few writers achieve during their lifetimes.

Since Fitzgerald's death, critics and readers have come to see his work and his life as dramatizations not simply of "The Twenties," but of American culture itself. And from his very weaknesses, no less than from his strengths, from an imagination and romantic sensibility which-as Edmund Wilson has remarked-lacked "intellectual control," F. Scott Fitzgerald drew a portrait of his time which is also a definition of our time, and a portrait of his people which perhaps has more meaning today than ever before.

THIS SIDE OF PARADISE

TEXTUAL ANALYSIS

BOOK I

Many critics have complained, with justice, that a great flaw in *This Side of Paradise* (aside from its loose, rambling structure) is the fact that the author seems uncertain as to his own attitude. He mocks the romantic delusions or emotional melodrama of his "little rich boy," Amory Blaine, while too often he shares, or seems to share, in the delusions themselves.

There is, in short, a kind of "smart" pseudo-sophistication imbedded within the narrative itself-a series of "clever comments" inserted for the sake of the cleverness rather than for any aesthetic purpose. And one result of this aesthetic self-indulgence is that the reader may find it difficult to take either Amory or his adventures with any degree of seriousness at all. Indeed, one feels as though the author himself were doing what Amory does during the course of the narrative: he merely holds the posture of writing about what actually is a very slight matter.

GESTURE WITHOUT SUBSTANCE

The need for some sort of imposing or melodramatic gesture is, of course, one of the chief qualities of Amory Blaine as an adolescent. That neither Amory nor his creator-F. Scott Fitzgerald-ever grew out of this need, is a fact that readers of Fitzgerald's works have recognized as central to the direction of his life and career. For Amory, at any rate, and for his mother Beatrice Blaine as well, the posture of reality all too often replaces reality itself, while gesture stands as a substitute for emotional commitment.

A woman of inherited wealth, Beatrice Blaine is a lovely, charming, superficial, childlike woman who maintains the posture of romance, a mere surface superimposed upon an essentially frigid or infantile refusal to commit herself to anything at all. She is, of course, the prototype for what has come to be known as the "Fitzgerald Woman" - an "enchanting" but essentially parasitic femme fatale whom Fitzgerald the author used so often for his books, and whom (in the person of Zelda) Fitzgerald the man finally married.

THE 'MOMMA'S BOY'

Beatrice's attitude toward the Church, for example, is typical of her attitude toward all emotional commitments. "She had once been a Catholic," we are told, "but discovering that the Priests were infinitely more attentive when she was in the process of either losing or regaining faith in the Mother Church, she maintained an enchantingly wavering attitude. . . . Next to doctors, priests were her favorite sport." The effect, of course, is that of a woman for whom all action is a matter of calculated performance.

Her very marriage to the weak and "ineffectual" (though rather literary and "romantic") Stephen Blaine, Amory's father, was a similar "sport": having married the all but invisible Mr. Blaine, Beatrice is subsequently rather astonished at actually becoming pregnant, and makes of Amory himself a perpetual toy of whatever fashionable manner she currently approves. That Amory, indeed, falls into a posture of play-acting whenever he is with Beatrice, is itself an indication of her "charm" - and her lack of substance.

The first chapter of *This Side of Paradise* is a very important one because it includes many **themes** which Fitzgerald repeats and amplifies throughout the rest of the novel. Amory, for example, from the very beginning of the book-especially during his early adolescence in Minneapolis and his four years at St. Regis' Academy in Connecticut-is precocious, "romantic," and literally stuffed with gestures that come both from his own rather exotic reading, and from the rootless globe-trotting of his mother. The very title of the chapter ("Amory, Son of Beatrice") is both a **parody** of **Epic** genealogy, and clear indication that Amory is a "momma's boy" in a very profound sense of the term.

Amory himself, with his long-lashed and unusual green eyes, with his calculated "charm," and his immense, though vague conviction of his own "superiority," from the very beginning relates to all aspects of reality through a veil of deliberate posturing. Anything too "real," indeed, alarms rather than interests him: while playing a romantic scene with Myra St. Clair, for example, he is enchanted with the young girl until he actually kisses her. And then occurs an abrupt change from "romantic" mood ("their lips brushed like wild flowers in the wind," writes Fitzgerald) to one of actual repugnance: Amory, having touched the actual flesh of the girl, feels merely a "sudden revulsion . . . disgust, loathing of the entire incident."

THE IDEAL OF ROMANCE

It is not the actual "kiss" which Amory desires (just as, later in his life, it is not sex itself which he wants), but rather it is the idea of being able to kiss the girl that intrigues him. He is, in short, perpetually fascinated with some imagined and usually baroque shadow of Grand Romance. And this Romance-whether of love, or "success," or "social justice," or "art" or "intellectual pursuits," or "religion" - simply collapses at any touch of sordid reality.

Amory Blaine, kissing Myra in the first chapter of *This Side of Paradise*, or desperately regurgitating slogans of political radicalism in the last chapter of the book, conveys the same sense of lack of substance: if, as the critic Edmund Wilson suggests, Amory's "revolt" at the end of the novel is a rebellion directed at nothing and one that goes nowhere, it is also true that his emotions are generally in the same condition.

For Amory Blaine, in short, any sort of actual consummation is necessarily sordid, somehow unsatisfying, always incomplete, and for this reason his career becomes a series of gestures which are aimed at appearance rather than at achievement. The achievement, indeed, is itself the deadliest "failure" of all: so long as Amory can suffer the pangs of "Great Love" without actually getting the girl, so long as he is prevented from actually achieving reality (prevented, preferably, by some sort of conditions which are themselves melodramatic-lack of money, perhaps, or Noble Sacrifice of some sort, or a "fine" reservation of conscience, or the invasion of previously Sacred Traditions by barbarian hordes with alien names), he can take a certain amount of pleasure from failure itself.

FAILURE AS A THEME

Failure emerges as a basic **theme** of *This Side of Paradise* - and of Fitzgerald's work as a whole. Inevitably, such failure marks the career of a "superior" person who, unable to cope with the demands of that reality which his own actions have created, falls back upon some Thwarted Dream of Beauty (either of moral value or Grand Passion) and so redeems the failure itself. The advantage, of course, is that failure permits the **protagonist** to maintain his "superiority" unchallenged by the demands of achievement. The burdens of reality, after all, are multiplied rather than lightened by the consummation of one's desire.

It is always more difficult to maintain a happy marriage than to marry one's Golden Girl; it is more difficult to offer creative leadership than to acquire a status of political importance; it is more difficult to become a poet than to have a Poetic Soul; it is more difficult to live with the healthy woman one has created from a beautiful neurotic, than to make the "cure" itself.

There is, in short, a certain fascination with what might be called the comforts of failure (or inability to cope with success) common to books like *Tender is the Night*, *The Great Gatsby*, and *This Side of Paradise*; in each case, Fitzgerald gives us a protagonist for whom consummation itself becomes destructive - an individual who in some way cannot commit himself totally to the reality of his own desires.

Amory Blaine, certainly, in his career up until the time he enters Princeton (Chapter I of *This Side of Paradise* carries us through Amory's 18th year), never seems quite "at home" even- or especially-when he does succeed in achieving a particular desire. Dreaming of "romance," he despises the flesh when it is finally offered to him. Obsessed with social success, and "showing off" either in the classroom or on the football field in order to achieve it, he seems almost determined to ruin the success itself, and acts in such a way as to alienate precisely those whom he has been trying so desperately to impress. Possessed of a fine intellect, he concentrates this intellect "on matters of popularity, a university social system, as represented by Biltmore teas and Hot Springs golf links."

FUTILITY AND DESIRE

The paradox of Amory Blaine, indeed, is the paradox of Fitzgerald himself. There is a group of opposing powers which, struggling in the same individual, produces a high pitch of frenzied activity leading, finally, to self-neutralization, or self-immolation, and so producing nothing at all: a kind of ineffectuality created not by lack of power, but rather by the multi-directional proliferation of power in terms of romance and perpetual "desire."

Amory senses this fatal "propensity toward failure" in himself. Speaking to a companion during his last year at St. Regis', he attempts to differentiate between the "philosophers" and the "slickers" of the campus world-which is, of course, a microcosm of the American world itself. The "slickers" are those individuals whose brilliance is concentrated solely on social (and therefore material) "success": they are the perpetual "in" people, the skilled "Big Men on Campus" who instinctively "know who to know," who concentrate their powers and make their emotions, their talents, their resources into effective and well-sharpened instruments of their will.

The "philosophers," on the other hand, are those who pursue their own course independently of the rewards - and the demands - of "Society" itself. And it is significant to note that Amory remarks that there is, in his own personality, much of both the "slicker" and the "philosopher."

Amory Blaine, indeed, who even as a youth "wondered how people could fail to notice that he was a boy marked for glory," was too much of a "slicker" to commit himself to his intellectual pursuits and aesthetic sensitivities; and too much of a "philosopher" to become a wholly successful "slicker." And this tension, so basic to F. Scott Fitzgerald's own life, is the central tension of Amory Blaine.

AMORY AT PRINCETON

Even at Princeton, Amory's schizophrenic ambitions tend to dilute and weaken whatever intellectual power he possesses. He loves and is awed by all things Princetonian-especially the traditions, the self-assurance, the air of "good breeding" that seem as much a part of campus environment as are the lecture halls and athletic fields. But the Princeton "atmosphere" rests on a foundation of intense social competition; Amory, indeed, discovers all too rapidly a pecking-order of prestige and power. It is, Fitzgerald tells us, a "breathless social system, that worship, seldom named, never really admitted, of the bogey 'Big Man.'"

Amory, of course, is fascinated with all the jockeying for "position." In a world composed of the "ins" and the "outs," he determines to achieve status at all costs, and to this end will use every talent at his disposal-whether it be a talent for "correct" dress, a talent for football, or a talent for writing. Each of these things, in short-the important along with the trivial-becomes little more than a method of achieving "success." For Amory Blaine, however, "success" is defined simply by the standards of the most powerful of those already established; lacking the kind of identity and will which enable young men like Burne Holiday to set the pattern for others, or to ignore all patterns in pursuit of goals shaped by personal rather than "social" goals, Amory simply drifts into "success" and, with an equal lack of conviction, drifts into failure as well.

ROMANCE AND LOVE

Even his relationships with women are defined by characteristic posturing. Isabelle Borge, for example, with whom he carries on a largely verbal "affair" and to whom he sends long and "rapturous" letters, is simply an image or dream-audience reflecting Amory's own narcissistic performances; their "love" is absurd because it is not real and cannot become real on the terms which Amory himself sets for it. The power of sex, indeed, offends him while it attracts; obsessed with guilt produced by his own emotions, Amory must either turn the emotions into Romantic Love derived from adolescent vaporing's, or "worship" their object (as he worships Clara Page) until reality in some way becomes purer than its own existence.

It is Clara Page, who-refusing to be turned into an object by Amory's emotional unreality-defines what is, perhaps, his essential weakness, and the weakness of the Fitzgerald Hero as a type. "You lack judgment," says Clara, "the judgment to decide at once when you know your imagination will play you false, given half a chance." For Clara perceives that Amory Blaine does not simply oppose reality with his own Idealism, but rather confuses one with the other, so that reality is virtually reshaped according to a dream-image that will be "spoiled" by any sort of real consummation. The result, inevitably, is a continual disaffection with reality, together with an equally persistent dissatisfaction with the Ideal.

Unwilling or unable to sacrifice "real" success by committing himself fully to an ideal, and unwilling to sacrifice his Ideals or Dream-roles by committing himself totally to the real world, Amory fluctuates between both, and finally can identify neither. And so he is left without emotional or intellectual direction-until the war provides at least a temporary solution by eliminating the need for any commitment whatever.

THIS SIDE OF PARADISE

TEXTUAL ANALYSIS

BOOK II

Although The Great Crusade served to provide Amory Blaine, and thousands of young gentlemen like him, with the illusion of purpose and Noble Cause, it was not long before the excitement generated by the Crusade itself settled down into The Great Hangover; by the end of the twenties, indeed, when Depression replaced both The New Sophistication and speakeasy Prohibition, the "fresh" vintage of the postwar years had turned into vinegar. Meanwhile, however, America-which had entered the war as though it were a Crusade-entered the years of peace expecting a Party.

AFTER THE WAR

The twenties, in short, were indeed remarkable, colorful, and schizophrenic years, and Book II of *This Side of Paradise* captures much of the essential quality of this memorable period. Along with political and social "disillusion" there was hope for some sort of "revolution" in politics, in the arts, and in moral codes; a romantic "pessimism" was combined with an equally romantic optimism, and both were infused with a pseudo-sophistication and "smartness" which themselves were grounded upon political and moral innocence.

The progress of Amory Blaine through his "Great Love" for Rosalind Connage - another Fitzgerald "Golden Girl" - and his subsequent despair, melodramatic posturing, wild dreams of expiation and/or radicalism, is itself the profile of an age. Rosalind herself, of course, is a vital element in this progress; a symbol of everything "beautiful" and "charming" and ultimately destructive in American values, she, like Daisy Buchanan in *The Great Gatsby* and Nicole Diver in *Tender is the Night*, is a creature of impulse rather than choice, and of sentiment rather than emotion; at once goddess and child, she destroys those who worship her and exploits those who love her.

ROSALIND: THE 'VAMPIRE'

Rosalind (whom Amory meets at the home of his Princeton friend, Alec Connage) is indeed the embodiment of the femme fatale of the Twenties-the "vampire" or Vamp who uses sex as a weapon, and "love" as an instrument of her own will, or rather, her own impulse. Lovely, spoiled, charming, "boyish" and yet womanly, she is-as Fitzgerald remarks-a "delicious" creature who somehow embarks upon Love as though it were a battle campaign, with the hapless male the only object worth pillaging.

Rosalind is one of a long series of Fitzgerald females, all of whom possess the charm, the lack of substance, and (ultimately) the destructiveness of poisoned lollypops. There is indeed,

Fitzgerald tells us, a great personal magnetism to this Golden Girl: "Her fresh enthusiasm," he says, "her will to grow and learn, her endless faith in the inexhaustibility of romance, her courage and fundamental honesty-these things are not spoiled." The very qualities which do make Rosalind so attractive, however, while they have not yet been "spoiled," are postulated upon a worship of false values and illusions, as though life itself were a series of "coming out" parties or masquerade balls. And it is this quality of non-reality defined by Cecelia, Rosalind's younger sister, when she remarks that for Rosalind all actions are merely roles to be played in a melodrama of her own invention.

BAUBLES AND TOYS

The point is that Rosalind never does "think" about money; she simply uses it-it is, necessarily, always there, hers by right and nature. "Thinking" about money would be sordid; she is not "interested" in money-merely in the baubles and pretty "toys" and charming willfulness that money itself makes possible. And her attitude toward money, furthermore, very much resembles her attitude toward "love" as well; Rosalind (like "the Fitzgerald Woman" in general) is not especially interested in passion, but rather in the tribute and sentiment she can exact by means of "winning" in the game of love, a "game" in which actual emotion is both distrusted and despised.

One of Rosalind's own remarks is, perhaps, the fullest revelation of her character - and one of the most remarkable lines in the book. Reproaching Amory for being rather too solemn in his protestations of love, she remarks: "I want sentiment, real sentiment - and I never find it." In this line, indeed, is summed up all the beautiful and lost and dreaming idealists of Fitzgerald's works. For what Rosalind demands is that "sentiment" in some way be made "real." By definition, of course, sentiment is the very antithesis of reality, and it is this confusion between sentiment and emotion, between "wish" and reality, that defines not only Rosalind, but the other Fitzgerald "Golden Girls" and the hapless men who become their lovers - and their victims.

That Amory himself shares rather than opposes Rosalind's "romanticism" is precisely why he can be so deeply hurt by her. For Amory too, the wish is - or should be - the father of reality. For Amory too there is a vision of "love" without flesh, of "wealth" without work; even in his attitude toward literature, for example, he admits that he cannot write because when he does try to write stories he is "distracted" both by the fear that he is "missing" life, and by an imaginative self-indulgence in fantasies and glories to be made possible by the writing itself.

THE ENJOYMENT OF FAILURE

Even in his despair, however, Amory is, in a sense, enjoying the melodrama of his own failure; his "loss," in other words, becomes simply one more possibility for vicarious experience: that is, experience without the demands and the sordid efforts which would be made necessary by consummation, and by reality. It is for this reason that he retreats so rapidly from Eleanor Savage, the girl he meets six months after the break with Rosalind. Eleanor makes the fatal mistake of demonstrating that she is a real human being possessed of real struggles and real spiritual substance; Amory "loves" her only so long as they can enjoy an "enchanted" summer - and at the first hint of reality, he runs from her like a panic-stricken adolescent.

Even his "sacrifice" for Alec Connage is based upon this fatal appetite for vicarious "experience" which is no experience at all: having taken Alec's place and been apprehended by hotel detectives to avoid a scandal which would hurt Alec's family, Amory searches-with great fascination-for the newspaper account of his own "disgrace." Once again he has managed to acquire a secondhand "reality" through a posture or role.

By the end of the novel, it is clear that the "failure" of Amory Blaine, like his hopes and dreams, must be considered one more gesture among many. His radical "philosophy" expounded in the last scene, his "love" and his "suffering," all have a peculiarly unfocused quality, as though his convictions, like his emotions, lack any cause or object, and for this reason exist merely for their own expression. It is precisely this lack of focus, however-this lack of emotional no less than intellectual substance-which is indeed so characteristic of the America which F. Scott Fitzgerald saw developing. Idealism without ideals; rhetoric without conviction; "love" without emotion-it is all there; and in Amory's final statement of "prophecy" or vision, there is the raw material from which Fitzgerald was to shape some of his finest work.

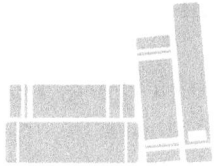

THIS SIDE OF PARADISE

CHARACTER ANALYSES

AMORY BLAINE

The central **protagonist** of *This Side of Paradise*, Amory incorporates many of the qualities associated with the "Fitzgerald Hero" - and indeed, with F. Scott Fitzgerald himself. Although possessed of a "good intellect" and great personal sensitivity, Amory is torn between his desire for Ideal values, and his worship of social success. Too often, indeed, Amory's dreams seem to absorb the real world, so that reality itself becomes, for him, little more than a means of achieving some vaguely imagined "ecstasy" of social "importance," or "love," or "sacrifice."

Amory, in short, is weakened rather than strengthened by his "Ideals" because the ideals themselves are grounded upon a kind of romantic inability to cope with the challenge of reality- the demands which are inevitably a part of the consummation of one's desires. For this reason he is attracted by the desire rather by its achievement; a boy for whom life tends to be a series of gestures or sentiments, he becomes a man for whom actual emotion, or commitment, is a source of danger rather than gratification. Amory, in short, "takes up" various roles, or appearances, but remains unwilling to fulfill the real demands created by the roles themselves. In a basic sense, he relates to all action-his writing, his "love affairs," even his failures-as though they were elements in a melodrama of his own creation.

Whether at St. Regis' Academy, or at Princeton, or during his essentially futile career after the war (when he falls in love with Rosalind Connage), Amory is unable to commit himself fully to any direction at all, and so dissipates his emotional and intellectual energy without "arriving" at a goal. A romantic who insists upon transmuting reality into the terms of his own romance, Amory confuses desire with reality, and so is unable to achieve satisfaction with the one, and remains unable to master the other.

BEATRICE BLAINE

Amory's mother, the first of a long line of "Fitzgerald women." Having inherited considerable wealth, Beatrice is a lovely, charming, superficial, childlike woman who maintains the posture of romance, a mere surface super-imposed upon an essentially frigid or infantile refusal to commit herself to anything at all. She is, in short, the "enchanting" but essentially parasitic femme fatale whom Fitzgerald the author used so often in his books, and whom (in the person of Zelda) Fitzgerald the man finally married.

THIS SIDE OF PARADISE

ESSAY QUESTIONS AND ANSWERS

Question: Who are the three "Fitzgerald Women" in *This Side of Paradise*?

Answer: The "Fitzgerald Woman" refers to a type of lovely, charming, childlike, and essentially parasitic "Golden Girl" that Fitzgerald used for many of his works. Infatuated with the idea of "romance" and exploiting rather than using her man, the "Fitzgerald Woman" is a creature whose lack of personal responsibility is based upon a view of life as a "party," a view of love as mere gesture, and an inability to cope with real emotion or real problems. Acting a series of "roles" in place of true commitment to anything or anyone, the "Golden Girl" nevertheless uses men and "ideas" as instruments to secure admiration, to achieve personal freedom from "sordid details," and to maintain her own position of freedom to indulge her own impulses.

In *This Side of Paradise*, the three women who fall into this "type," are Beatrice Blaine, Amory's mother; Isabel Borge, his first "serious" love (whom he met while at Princeton), and Rosalind Connage, the sister of a Princeton friend, who shared a Grand Passion with Amory after the war. Beatrice-who shaped much of Amory's character-is a person for whom all commitments are essentially impulses calculated to gain attention and a kind of spurious excitement; Isabel is a "speed" whose facade of romantic posturing covers (as it does with most of the "Fitzgerald Women") an essential emotional frigidity; and Rosalind is an "expensive proposition" whose "romance" is itself based upon romantic gestures, and freedom from all true responsibility or emotion.

Question: In what way does Amory's Princeton experience define his basic character - and the weakness of what has come to be known as the "Fitzgerald Hero"?

Answer: During his career at Princeton (and even earlier, during his school days at St. Regis'), Amory demonstrates the lack of focus, the lack of emotional and intellectual direction which, together with a pervading "romantic" view of reality, virtually insures the kind of "failure" so often associated with Fitzgerald's central protagonists. Viewing life as a kind of melodrama, or series of mere "roles," Amory is unable to commit himself fully to any single goal or standard of values; his very talents, whether for football or literature, become means rather than ends, a method of securing public approval and "position." Amory, in short, is attracted by - and ultimately defines life as - the appearance of "success," rather than its substance; lacking any true commitment even to his own avowed purposes, he tends to fear the demands and the challenges of any true consummation, and dilutes his own powers by a vacillating and "dreamy" confusion between desire and reality.

Question: What are the main structural difficulties of *This Side of Paradise*?

Answer: *This Side of Paradise* is a very loosely constructed novel, actually a series of **episodes** rather than a carefully worked narrative. Continuity is provided by the figure and the "education" (or rather, the development) of Amory Blaine; it is his various crises, moral revelations, and insecurities which "tie up" the structure of the book, and also serve as a kind of dramatization of the aimless "war generation" as a whole.

A serious problem, however, is the fact that Fitzgerald often seems uncertain as to his own attitude toward Amory and the people surrounding him; he mocks the romantic delusions or emotional melodrama of his "little rich boy" (Amory), while too often he shares, or seems to share, in the delusions themselves. There is, in short, a kind of self-indulgence in the narrative itself, a "smart" pseudo-sophistication which often serves no aesthetic purpose, and is actually distracting to the reader. And yet it is also true that this quality, itself so distracting, was characteristic of the Twenties as a period - and in this sense, the very lack of narrative focus of *This Side of Paradise* can be viewed as serving a dramatic purpose.

Question: Why is Amory Blaine's concept of "success" (like that of other Fitzgerald Heroes) often considered representative of basic patterns within American culture?

Answer: Amory's concept of "success" is itself a kind of vaguely glowing "Ideal" whose basis is romance rather than reality. Almost pathetically concerned with "belonging" to whatever sources of power happen to be in control of his environment at a particular time, Amory is at the same time scornful of those whose sole motivation is social approval. It is this tension-the tension between his desire to "belong" and his desire to be "himself" (or, as he puts it, to be a "personage" rather than a mere "personality"), that causes much of Amory's difficulty in fully committing himself to anything at all.

"Success" itself, furthermore, for Amory Blaine, is largely a matter of achieving some vaguely defined "happiness" without the demands and the sordid details of reality. Unwilling to risk social "failure" on one hand, and fearful of concentrating on actual work for the sake of the work itself, Amory is left floundering in a never-never land of feverish dreams, shadowy guilts, and glowing desires. Material success, in short, is always subordinated to some "dream of ecstasy" - while the dream, purged of all commitment, results in an emotional vacuum and perpetual ache of disaffection.

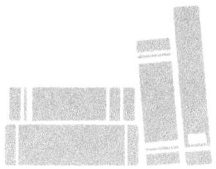

TENDER IS THE NIGHT

CRITICAL COMMENTARY

D. W. Harding, in his perceptive essay on *Tender is the Night*, remarks that Fitzgerald's **protagonist** in his last completed novel is a "tragic child-hero whom no one is great enough to help." For Dick Diver, brilliant psychiatrist and physician, brilliant husband (or rather, guardian) of a brilliantly wealthy and beautiful neurotic, is indeed a perpetual resource for those about him. So completely is he available to be used by others, that he is ultimately quite used up, consumed by an essentially parasitic world whose moral weakness feeds upon moral strength, until the strength itself is broken. And when this happens, when the "goodness" of Dick Diver is no longer needed (and when his own control and power have been sufficiently drained), there can be no question of returning the favor: Dick Diver exists to help rather than to be helped, to be used rather than use. And so he is, ultimately, discarded like an empty medicine bottle.

THE 'IDEAL' OF SERVICE

Certainly Dick Diver's role as "physician" is essential to the novel. He exists, as Nicole Diver's wealthy sister points out, to serve a function: that, indeed, is what he has been "paid" for. It is Nicole's wealth, after all, that to a great extent has made possible Dick's grace, his manners, his mastery of the entire "carnival by the sea" atmosphere which he enjoys, and which he is entitled to enjoy as a condition of his service. Once this service no longer "pays off" - when the "cure" is completed and when Dick has given all he has to give - the "contract" is cancelled and the physician-husband is simply discharged with gratitude, with some regret, and with considerable embarrassment when the physician himself demonstrates the poor taste of developing weaknesses of his own. In a sick room, after all, the function of the patient is not to take the pulse of the serviceable specialist he has hired.

In the moral sick room of the postwar world, Dick Diver finds himself surrounded by "love" which is indeed the product of disease rather than health, and as he proceeds with his various "cures" - as he expends the moral and personal energy at his disposal-his own deterioration becomes inevitable. For Dick Diver, who agreed to make one of his patients his wife (and so contract for exclusive services), forgets that his wife is, primarily, his patient. He makes the fatal error in any such relationship: that is, he fails to remain objective enough, and confuses functional with emotional commitment.

Having contracted to cure Nicole, he offers her whatever is necessary to achieve the cure itself, including - and in this lies his fatal weakness - his love. Having offered his love, moreover, he expects her loyalty in return, but fails to remember that whatever loyalty she is able to give, is itself the product of the condition he has been attempting to cure. When the patient is well, there simply is no reason for loyalty at all, and any insistence upon it is rather embarrassing.

MORALITY AS WEAKNESS

In the work of F. Scott Fitzgerald, there is repeated insistence that-given the nature of the moral wasteland-love itself must be a source of weakness rather than strength. Lovers, indeed, can only survive when they understand that love is primarily a matter of exchange - an exchange of one sort of currency or another, a contract which depends upon the fulfillment of particular conditions. When the conditions (or one of the lovers) change, the contract is, in a sense, cancelled: emotional commitment itself becomes an irrelevancy.

It is this realization which Fitzgerald's protagonists, inevitably romantic Idealists in a world in which "romance" itself represents the very antithesis of Idealism, fail to understand completely, and so create their own destruction. Amory Blaine, for example, in *This Side of Paradise*, fails to understand that the very basis of his love with Rosalind, his Fairy Princess, must be an "enchanted" love or it is nothing; "enchantment" is the very basis of its existence, and to ask of a Fairy Princess that she become a struggling housewife must be a contradiction in terms, a violation of the original contract. Given the moral wasteland, and the exploitation which lies at the very center of all "romance" in the Wasteland, it is Amory rather than Rosalind who becomes absurd as he insists upon commitments which had never really been included in the original "contract" at all.

So too a **protagonist** like Jay Gatsby forgets that his very role as a lover is defined by the lack of substance of the role itself; for Daisy Buchanan he represents the possibility of a particular kind of romantic "glow" which must be darkened and finally dissipated at the first puff of reality. It is, indeed, Jay Gatsby's "function" to keep such reality away from Daisy, and when, for any reason, he is not able to do so, the conditions of the contract change, the "bargain" is no longer in effect, "all bets is off" and Daisy returns to her husband-whose direct and brutal management of reality represents another kind of "bargain" altogether, but one which he is quite capable of keeping.

NICOLE AS EXPLOITER

So too, in *Tender is the Night*, Dick Diver is not so much deserted by Nicole, as eliminated by her when the original conditions of their relationship no longer apply; one might say, indeed, that he is cancelled along with their "contract." For having recovered her strength and health, a kind of hardness of Will defined by Dick himself at the end of the book when he observes that she has become good "Georgia pine, which is the hardest wood known, except lignum vitae from New Zealand," Nicole is free to choose, or rather be chosen, by a man who in his own right represents (just as Tom Buchanan in *The Great Gatsby* represents) an exploiter rather than a creator of "love." Nicole, indeed, no longer wishes or has need of a man who is "always right" in his relations with her or in his facade of mannered perfection which he holds before the world. Given the fact that she has recovered her own Self, so perfect a diagnostician is simply no longer necessary, and so she takes a man who uses what Dick Diver first creates and then (unfortunately) actually loves.

THE USERS AND THE USED

Dick Diver, of course, is, by the end of the book, no longer "always right" at all, and this in itself would be grounds for the "cancellation of contract" between them. Having taken all through their relationship, Nicole suddenly finds herself in the position of having to give emotional support, or first aid, to her own physician; this is manifestly unfair and unprofitable, and-hard as "Georgia pine" once again, she turns to Tommy Barban, the "realist" of sound calculations and direct appetites.

With Tommy, there need be no question of Ideal aside from act, and no question of Loyalty aside from function. With some sentimental regret, and with some pity as well, Nicole turns from the depleted resources of Dick to the sleek, powerful, efficient, pragmatic "hardness" of a man who is indeed morally Dick's inferior, and so-in all other terms-necessarily more functional and less "risky." And for Nicole, like most of Fitzgerald's female protagonists, risk is the ultimate sin, and a kind of functional pragmatism or freedom of impulse the ultimate virtue; with Dick Diver there would be too much of the one, and not enough of the other.

Tommy, indeed, even in his "admiration" for Dick at the beginning of the novel, is admiring not the man, but the physician; his indignant "protection" against any sort of interference with the Dick-Nicole relationship is the perception of weakness rather than the acknowledgement of strength. Tommy insists that no distracting sordidness must be allowed to interfere with this "ideal marriage" because he understands clearly that the process of the marriage itself is one of exploitation rather than love; when Nicole is "ready" for him (that is, when she is "cured" and has no further need for the medication provided by Dick, medication which-on his part-so foolishly, almost childishly, turns into love), Tommy will reappear and take what never really belonged to Dick Diver at all.

AN AMBIGUOUS MARRIAGE

Ironically, Tommy's estimate of the Divers' marriage is in many ways more firmly based upon reality than is the weight of emotional commitment which Dick attempts to place upon it. For one thing, the central trauma of Nicole's life-the incestuous relationship with her own father-resulted in a fixation dramatized as well as ultimately cured by her relationship with Dick. What she "sees" in Dick, in other words, or rather what she requires from him, is at once more ambiguous and less definable than any simple process of emotional "cure."

There is, in short, a certain element of transference in Nicole's attitude toward her husband, who, in his role of husband no less than in his function as psychiatrist, "takes up the burden" of Nicole's father in more ways than one. Nicole's father, of course, like Tommy, is one of the users of the world; having created a particular crisis, he simply uses the particular skill and moral strength of Dick to solve the problems involved. When Dick marries his problem as well as treats it, he-in a very basic sense-compounds the condition he set out to cure.

As a psychiatrist, of course, Dick knows this and is warned quite clearly and quite forcefully that his marriage to Nicole is (from a professional standpoint) a violation of all those carefully structured values to which, as a physician, he himself had been committed. From a personal standpoint, his marriage to Nicole is even more dangerous; becoming something of a "father-figure" to a woman whose relations with her father had been so shattering, Dick embarks upon a "love" in which emotions are very murky indeed-emotions, furthermore, which depend for their support upon a framework of perfection and strengths normally attributed to a parent rather than a husband.

A WASTE OF VIRTUE

In a sense, then, Dick creates for himself a situation in which his own "infallibility," his own "goodness" and "perfection," serves as a framework, or bulwark, for emotional and moral unhealth, and once again, as in so much of Fitzgerald's work, we have a **protagonist** whose very virtues are directed (or are used) for the perpetuation of everything to which they are ostensibly opposed. One might almost say that Dick dooms himself to play the "father-figure" in two directions: one, the result of psychic trauma (Nicole's incestuous relationship with her father), can be "cured" only at the cost of possible destruction of the physical basis of his marriage; the other-his role as Perfect Parent-must be destroyed when he demonstrates his own weakness or lack of perfection. Either way, Dick Diver, in so many ways the "Fitzgerald Hero" despite his moral superiority to those about him, has built his own Enchanted Palace on a swamp.

Dick's virtues, furthermore, are diluted by a fatal lack of that "toughness" or dedication to one's own code which alone can help a man shape his life according to his own convictions. Faced with any sort of need, or pressured by any sort of personal appeal, Dick uses his very Idealism not as a means to shape reality, but rather as a reason for avoiding it. The fact that Rosemary "loves" him, or rather, requires him to serve as her selfless and gentle tutor in the process of her own development, makes Dick's involvement with her all but inevitable; unable to say "no" to the Ideal Purity of his own selflessness, perpetually sacrificing his own standards for noble and ideal reasons, Dick is, finally, indeed "too good to be true."

THE 'TRAGIC CHILD'

In this sense, Dick Diver is a child rather than a man, and it is this quality of childishness which makes Dick's "tragedy" a matter of pathos rather than power. Like Jay Gatsby, who attempts to "fulfill his Platonic conception of himself" by surbordinating all means to some vaguely perceived Ideal of Beauty, Dick attempts to fulfill an equally "Platonic" conception: the Ideal of Pure Goodness. And also like Gatsby, who must be destroyed by his own purity (since the Ideal, by definition, cannot be both owned and worshipped), Dick destroys for himself the possibility of any real relationship, or love, precisely because Pure Goodness makes any such "reward" unthinkable.

Devoted to the Ideal of Service, Dick responds only to those situations in which he can achieve the moral superiority of serving - those situations in which he himself is "loved" only as long as he serves. At the same time, however, he becomes exhausted enough to demand that he be loved "for himself along" -quite apart from any service he is able to render. The result, obviously, is a kind of self-created contradiction or impossibility. Like Amory Blaine, who first creates the Ideal and then despises the reality of emotional consummation, Dick Diver creates precisely those situations which virtually guarantee his own "disillusion."

"His position at the end," says D. W. Harding of Dick, "is the apotheosis of the hurt child saying 'nobody loves me,' but the child's self-pity and reproaches against the grown ups have been largely rooted out and in their place is a fluctuation between self-disgust and a conviction that this can happen to the nicest children." Even more pathetic than this "self-disgust," however, is the fact that "nobody loves" Dick Diver for very good reason: he has so arranged matters that he is indeed "loved" for his services rather than himself. And his "bitterness" as a result of this discovery hardly earns much sympathy.

When Dick, for example, understands that he can have Mary North by "helping" her (as he had "helped" Nicole, and Rosemary, and anyone else who had ever used him), the result is only a "bitter" laughter after which he makes the gesture of self-imposed exile. But certainly the reader may well ask of Dick Diver (as of Amory Blaine): how could he have expected anything else? For Dick, repeating the inevitable fear-of-consummation so notable throughout Fitzgerald's work, surrounds himself with his Ideal of Service just as Amory Blaine surrounds himself with an Ideal of Romance, and Jay Gatsby surrounds himself with an Ideal of Beauty.

Ultimately these various Ideals are themselves methods of insulation rather than commitment, methods of avoiding real love rather than achieving it. It is Tommy Barban, the man who makes no pretence of "earning love" through any Idealism, who takes love as it is and offers himself as he is, who ultimately does succeed in "getting the girl." If Tommy (like Tom Buchanan in *The Great Gatsby*), lacks the idealist dimension of Fitzgerald's "finer" heroes-heroes who are also losers-perhaps we can say that his heroes lack the strength, the will, and the knowledge of reality which enable such people as Tommy to "win out."

OBJECTIVE NARRATIVE

Most of the first section of *Tender is the Night* (that is, most of Book I) is narrated through the point of view of Rosemary Hoyt, a young, "dewy and still virginal movie actress possessed of a certain strength of will and personal soundness under a veneer of undefined romanticism." Rosemary, of course, provides the kind of objective "observer" which Fitzgerald needs if he is to render the peculiar kind of Idealism which at once serves to ennoble and destroy Dick Diver, and the very "special" world that Dick and Nicole have created.

Rosemary, indeed, serves as a means for setting up the surface of the "perfect" world of the Divers, before events force the surface itself to collapse. As she becomes "initiated" into the realities of Dick, Nicole, Tommy Barban, Abe North, and the others who make up the "circle" whom she first meets at the French Riviera ("the carnival by the Sea," as Fitzgerald was later to remark of his own experience with Zelda), and as she "loves" Dick Diver himself, there is a sense of some kind of emotional or moral disease beneath the enchantment, and the cleverness, and all the loveliness and charm of the Dick Diver world that deepens and intensifies. But even before we know precisely what this unhealth or illusion actually might be, there is strong emphasis on precisely those qualities which foreshadow events to come.

Part of this emphasis is achieved by the terms in which the characters are described either through Rosemary's point of view, the objective commentary of Fitzgerald as author, or "symbolic action" in which apparently insignificant details refer to definitive qualities or roles. An example of the latter method is the scene in which Nicole Diver, having arranged to meet Dick for a love-assignation, goes "shopping" with Rosemary, who is herself in love with the "perfect" young psychiatrist. As Nicole "buys things" with complete carelessness and a kind of wild "acquisitive impulse," what emerges is the portrait of a woman whose personal identity is defined primarily by her role as consumer, and this is indeed not only a basic role for Nicole Diver, but for the "Fitzgerald Woman" as a type.

THE 'REALIST'

Just as Nicole's role as consumer, as user, is foreshadowed by the early scenes of the book, so too Tommy Barban's direct and ruthless drive to power is defined both through Rosemary's point of view, and dramatic referral, in which comments made in one context actually define an important quality set up in another. For Tommy, as we first meet him (through Rosemary's impressions), is "unmistakably Latin," is lean, hard, practical, self-contained in his own appetites and own desires. There is little of the glow of Idealism that surrounds Dick Diver (as it does with the Fitzgerald Hero in general); he gives the impression of "bunched force," a kind of ferocity and will, and is somehow "less civilized" than the others.

Tommy, indeed, "likes" the Divers, "especially her" - and yet after being with Nicole and Dick, some inner pressure within himself forces him to "go to war." Certainly there is violence here (violence and Will define Tommy as the Ideal of Service defines Dick); and even more than violence, an impatience with any moral or intellectual idealism whatsoever. He is a mercenary soldier, and-as he explains to the hapless Albert McKisco, a rather ineffectual American "intellectual" with whom he later fights a "duel" to protect the Divers from scandal - "my business is to kill people."

There is a simplicity, and force, and stubborn stupidity about Tommy which indeed make up an impressive whole, for these qualities are themselves subordinated to the assertion of Will and appetite. And as he "protects" the Divers, as he serves as their "watch-dog," one feels that he is serving not them, but himself. Such is, of course, the case, for it is Tommy Barban who "takes" Nicole after she has consumed her husband and returned to "health"; it is Tommy who finally breaks the marriage he so forcefully "protects" early in the book. And in this connection, the remark of Dick Diver in quite another context, serves not only to define Tommy's role, but the nature of his own marriage as well. Refusing a screen test that Rosemary had arranged in a burst of adolescent enthusiasm, Dick remarks: "The strongest guard is placed at the gateway to nothing... Maybe because the condition of emptiness is too shameful to be divulged."

A SPIRITUAL VACUUM

By the end of Book I, at any rate, Rosemary - and the reader - has indeed been initiated into the moral and spiritual vacuum which exists beneath the surface of the "enchanted" Dick Diver world. Abe North, for example, the composer who after a period of creative genius has degenerated into an alcoholic failure, serves as counterpoint to Dick himself; both men are sensitive, noble, "fine," and flawed by a fatal weakness or inability to focus their virtues. Like Abe North, Dick Diver has exhausted his own talents on trivialities, has wasted his own disciplined will and education so that the result is not "work," but rather self-indulgence to an Ideal which is itself a triviality. It is significant that "Abe's "musical score" and Dick's "scientific book" are placed in the same category: they are both real labors that have been dissipated and finally destroyed by devotion to the same sort of "meretricious beauty" that turned the virtues of Jay Gatsby into a pathetic dream, and the intellectual and imaginative richness of Amory Blaine into a St. Vitus dance of perpetual adolescence.

Rosemary Hoyt, of course, later in the book "grows out" of her love for Dick; possessed of a firm, disciplined, and unwavering Will-to-reality, she develops into a woman, and for this reason can offer nothing to Dick Diver, who persists in replacing his own manhood with a role of his own creation-a role in which "perfection" and "youthfulness" and the Ideal of service actually serve as a kind of "enchanted circle" in which Dick attempts to avoid the challenge of reality.

A RETREAT FROM REALITY

So too does Nicole "outgrow" her husband; still requiring direction and will in her man, she finds that Dick is, after all, so fully devoted to his own nobility as a physician-father that he can be nothing else. And so Dick Diver sinks further and further into a morass of desperation and "demoralized" nobility; because he refuses to face the facts of his own decay, there is total failure of that Idealism which he had erected as a bulwark against futility. And in this connection, one might note that Dick's comments on World War I as the destruction of an entire value-structure, has much to do with his own "retreat" from reality itself.

Dick's "Idealism," at any rate, finally sinks from the weight of its own impossibilities, and the final result represents something more than the decay of a single individual or the break up of a single marriage. For in the story of Dick Diver we have still another dramatization of a system in which men become incapable of growing past an Ideal which is itself based upon a waste of original power, or rather the distortion of such power through a kind of perpetual adolescence. And this, of course, is the "story" which F. Scott Fitzgerald dramatized in his novels - and in so much of his own life.

TENDER IS THE NIGHT

ESSAY QUESTIONS AND ANSWERS

Question: Dick Diver has been called a "tragic child." Discuss the meaning of this phrase, and its application to *Tender is the Night*.

Answer: The very phrase "tragic child" is, in a basic sense, a contradiction in terms, and this to no small extent points up a paradox in the role of Dick Diver himself. For the Tragic Hero is by general definition a man great enough, and possessed of courage enough, to confront the necessary consequences of his own actions, and the reality upon which these actions are based. For Dick Diver, however, neither consequences nor reality are confronted at all; Dick, indeed, uses his very virtues and talents not to shape the real world, but rather to avoid it-to build an Ideal which itself serves as a kind of moral and emotional wish-fulfillment.

The fact that Dick is motivated by wish-fulfillment rather than choice of action is something more than a "Tragic Flaw"; it is a measure of his incapacity to reach any tragic dimension whatsoever. His vision of reality, in short, is less "flawed" by error, than it is filtered through - and distorted by - a refusal to commit himself to any relationship not based upon the Role which he has created for himself. In this sense he is indeed a "child," or at least a perpetual adolescent, and the lack of manliness and substance so basic to Dick as a **protagonist** is at best part of a larger "tragedy": the tragedy of an entire culture devoted to the substitution of Romance for reality, and of wish-fulfillment or impulse for choice.

Question: How does *Tender is the Night* represent an advance in narrative structure when compared to a novel like *This Side of Paradise*?

Answer: *This Side of Paradise*, the first of Fitzgerald's novels, is a brilliant but episodic work by a very young writer who too often sacrifices unity of effect and structure for a kind of aesthetic self-indulgence: that is, a kind of "storytelling" in which the author too often merely demonstrates his own cleverness with "smart" but irrelevant asides, observations, and episodes. In his first novel, moreover, Fitzgerald himself seems too "close" to his material; he both mocks and rhapsodizes over his own characters, and the result is a confused judgment - and a confused reaction on the part of the reader.

With *Tender is the Night*, however, Fitzgerald subordinates **episode** to total drama, and succeeds-as in *The Great Gatsby*- in making the drama itself a symbol of wider moral and social meaning. There is far less random "cleverness" than in *This Side of Paradise*; the cleverness itself, in other words, is subordinated to the purpose and meaning of the drama. By maintaining a certain objectivity, moreover, Fitzgerald avoids intruding into his own narrative. His use of Rosemary Hoyt's point of view, for example, serves at once to introduce the characters, to define

Rosemary herself, and to provide a dimension of **irony** to the subsequent dramatic development.

Question: Discuss Tommy Barban as a "Hero of the Moral Wasteland."

Answer: Like Tom Buchanan of *The Great Gatsby*, Tommy Barban is a man completely without Ideals; his only moral "code," indeed, is one of calculated self-interest, and the imposition of his own will in order to achieve the object of his own desires or appetites. A mercenary soldier whose "business is to kill," Tommy is a creature of violence-without-meaning; even his political "ideology" (if such a word can be applied to Tommy at all) is simply a matter of self-interest. So too Tommy's "protection" of Dick Diver and Nicole is a matter of calculation; understanding that Nicole "needs" Dick so long as she is ill, he also understands that Nicole will be ripe for the taking when Dick's "services" are no longer required.

Question: What Is Dick Diver's "Great betrayal"?

Answer: The great betrayal made by Dick Diver-the fatal action (or avoidance of action) which in a sense creates his own destruction-is the fact that he violates the commitments and ethics of real work for the sake of a false or romanticized "Ideal" of self-sacrifice. Like Jay Gatsby, who subordinates all ethics in pursuit of his Golden Girl, or like Amory Blaine (in *This Side of Paradise*) who subordinates consummation to adolescent romance, Dick Diver subordinates his own identity as a physician and a worker to a kind of "charm" and "service" which is at once false and self-perpetuating. Scorning real work and real life as somehow too "small" for his own dreams,

Dick ultimately fails as a physician and as a person-despite the fact that he is, in all respects, a "purer" individual than are the masters and manipulators of the moral wasteland-people like Tommy Barban, "Baby" Warren, or Nicole herself.

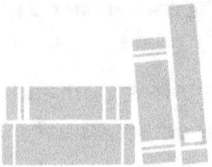

CRITICAL REVIEW

"I talk with the authority of failure," F. Scott Fitzgerald once wrote in his notebooks, soon after his break with Ernest Hemingway, "Ernest with the authority of success. We could never sit across the same table again." Whether or not Fitzgerald considered himself a "failure" in his own lifetime, however, one thing is clear: during the last decade, his reputation among literary critics and non-specialized readers has grown to the point where no study of American literature - and certainly no anthology of American literature - is complete without either a discussion or representation of his work.

THE QUESTION OF FITZGERALD'S "FAILURE"

The question of Fitzgerald's "failure" has been to a great extent the result of two elements in Fitzgerald's career: first, the fact that he did produce an enormous number of "slick" stories for the high-priced magazines, while two of his four novels (*This Side of Paradise* in 1920, and *The Beautiful and the Damned* in 1922) were "best sellers" from a financial, if not literary point of view.

Fitzgerald, in short, was preoccupied with financial success throughout his career, and much of his work was indeed produced with the market rather than the muse foremost in his mind. As Arthur Mizener points out, most of the 160 stories that Fitzgerald wrote between 1920 and (approximately) 1940 were frankly written for money. For this reason, if for no other, Fitzgerald's critical reputation was indeed vulnerable; literary critics have always tended to look askance at undue financial success (or preoccupation) on the part of literary artists, a fact which is obvious enough in the careers of such writers as John Steinbeck and Ernest Hemingway among many others.

The fact that Fitzgerald did produce a great deal of semi-hack writing, and the fact that he became a literary celebrity too early and too richly in his career, undoubtedly shaped critical attitudes toward his work. In addition to this aspect of the Fitzgerald career, however, there was also the fact that he became so thoroughly identified with the glittering world of flappers, disillusions, and "early sorrows" romantically a part of the mythology of the American twenties, that critics often seemed to be rendering a judgment not on Fitzgerald's work, but rather on the cultural environment which provided its raw material. The news-columnist Westbrook Pegler, for example, summed up this sort of blanket dismissal by referring to Fitzgerald as being both spokesman for and representative of a "group or cult of juvenile crying-drunks."

It is always dangerous, however, to confuse the **theme** which a writer uses for his work, with the status or value of the work itself. A novelist like Virginia Woolf, for example, is not to be considered aesthetically "sterile" merely because psychological and emotional sterility is a basic **theme** of her books. And if "failure" is a basic **theme** of F. Scott Fitzgerald, one must remember that he was attempting to render a society which had indeed "failed" precisely because of its universal preoccupation with "success."

That Fitzgerald himself illustrated this paradox-a worship of "success" so intense that it virtually insures a conviction of personal failure-in no way invalidates his artistic vision. On the contrary, the fact that Fitzgerald was so completely a man of his own time and own culture, explains to no small degree his ability to render cultural reality in his stories and novels.

Fitzgerald was not invulnerable to the American Dream of "success without sweat"; ironically (and sometimes bitterly) aware of his own "mixed motives" as an artist, he saw in himself precisely those moral and intellectual flaws which were shaping the direction of America as a nation. Granted that he was extremely sensitive to his times, one must remember that such a sensitivity is hardly a disadvantage to a literary artist. That Fitzgerald possessed this sensitivity enabled him to use in his work what the critic Glenway Wescott has called an "extreme environmental sense."

EARLY WORK

In his early work, however, Fitzgerald seemed to have the "environmental sense" without the aesthetic objectivity which alone serves to shape literature into something more than a reflection of prevailing intellectual or social modes. Quite aside from the financial and personal necessities which drove him to "selling big" to the "big markets," one might almost say that Fitzgerald had been too close to "his times"; that he had not yet succeeded in viewing the times themselves - and the tensions within himself so vitally characteristic of them - through a structuring of fiction which would stand alone, independent of fashionable literary posture, or current intellectual preoccupations, or personal anticipations in which the writer almost seems to view his own achievement before the work itself has been achieved.

This Side of Paradise, for example, which made Fitzgerald something of a literary celebrity in 1920 (and which, of course, enabled him to "earn" Zelda and build his own Golden Palace of "success") was attacked by literary critics on precisely these grounds: that it was far too completely a "mixed bag" of assorted literary modes, prevailing intellectual "smartness," moral exposes which themselves indicated a certain naivete on the part of the author, and a certain sophomoric anxiety to "shock" as well as please. As Heywood Broun rather dyspeptically remarked of the book: "There is too much footwork and too much feinting for anything solid and substantial being accomplished. You can't expect to have blood drawn in any such exhibition as that."

THE NEED FOR OBJECTIVITY

Critics were generally agreed that Fitzgerald's own enthusiasm as a story-teller, his own romanticism as a person, his own delight in the "smart" and topical, his own view of literature as a kind of "key" to the "good life," and his obvious debt to those writers (such as Tarkington, Wells, and others) who had been fashionable among Princeton undergraduates, resulted in a kind of grab-bag of literary mannerisms. There was, in short, general agreement that while Fitzgerald might be a brilliant addition to the American literary scene, he was as yet what Frederick Hoffman called a genius manque-a rather precocious young man who seemed to be playing a "brilliant" role in some drama of his own creation, a drama in which the novel itself was merely an episode.

The need for objectivity in Fitzgerald's work, the need for less self-conscious play-acting at literature and "being in the know," was a criticism reiterated by literary commentators such as Edmund Wilson, Paul Rosenfeld, and many others. Certainly Fitzgerald's first two novels are marked by a lack of what James E. Miller, Jr. calls the principle of selectivity; still very much the bright young author, Fitzgerald in *This Side of Paradise* and *The Beautiful and the Damned* (although to a somewhat lesser extent in the latter work) tends to sacrifice control and structure to a kind of pyrotechnic display of random witticisms, social observations, fashionable comment (or condescension), irrelevant "self-expression" - all the flaws, in short, of a young writer impressed with himself and with the need to be "successful" at least as much as he is impressed with the art of literature.

THE CRITICS AND GATSBY

With *The Great Gatsby* in 1925, however, this structural control was achieved-achieved through both the dual narrative we have already discussed (the technique, partly influenced by the novelist Joseph Conrad, of filtering action and meaning through a narrator at once involved with the action and commenting upon it), and through the use of "natural" symbols growing out of the action and situation of the story: the eyes of Doctor T. J. Eckleburg, for example, or the "green light" of Daisy Buchanan, or the "ritual of the silk shirts" in Gatsby's mansion. The book, in short, was praised by critics as a profound definition of the loss of American values-the loss of "The American Dream" - and a work of literary art in which ironic drama was all the more powerful for being controlled and absorbed within the substance of the work itself.

It was not so much that *The Great Gatsby* was (as Andrew Turnbull remarks) "less autobiographical" than Fitzgerald's earlier works, as it was that the autobiography had been used more relevantly to the fiction. In posing the "Jay Gatsby" part of his own vision against the "Nick Carroway" part, Fitzgerald had achieved the sort of objectivity which makes it possible for a novelist to "stay out of his book" - or rather, to let the book say what it has to say without intrusive explication. There is less of Fitzgerald "talking" to his readers as Fitzgerald than in either of his earlier novels, and this is also true of what most critics consider to be the novel ranking next to *Gatsby*: *Tender is the Night*, which appeared in 1934.

The Great Gatsby, at any rate, was highly praised; William Rose Benet, for example, in a *Saturday Review* essay, remarked that "for the first time Fitzgerald surveys the Babylonian captivity of this era unblinded by the bright lights," and commentators such as Malcolm Cowley, Dennis Hardy, James Thurber, Edmund Wilson, John Peale Bishop, and many others sensed a new substance in Fitzgerald's work.

CRITICAL RESERVATIONS

This is not to say that Fitzgerald had achieved any sort of literary apotheosis or Sainthood. The critical voices were by no means unanimous, even on the subject of *The Great Gatsby*; H. L. Mencken, for example, attacked both the novel (which he considered little more than an "anecdote") and its chief character, whom he considered so "vague" as to be a sort of disembodied shadow of a literary **protagonist**. *Tender is the Night* received mixed reviews, and there remained much critical feeling that F. Scott Fitzgerald had indeed "wasted" too much of his talent on unworthy projects, while personal difficulties (his own and

Zelda's) had wasted too much of him. Arthur Mizener remarks that as late as 1939, *The Great Gatsby* was dropped from the Modern Library because it "failed to sell."

FITZGERALD'S GROWING REPUTATION

After Fitzgerald's death, however, the tide shifted, and by the time Edmund Wilson had edited and published *The Crack-Up* in 1945, with serious critical essays, interest in Fitzgerald both as an individual and as a literary artist reached considerable proportions. *Gatsby* was reissued with a laudatory introduction by Lionel Trilling, and full-length studies soon were appearing, together with critical anthologies and many articles in both the scholarly and "middlebrow" magazines. Most of the significant criticism on Fitzgerald, indeed, is a product of the last two decades; his works have been reprinted in both softback and hard-cover editions; his stories and novels-especially *The Great Gatsby*-have been "rediscoverered" by academic and non-academic readers throughout the United States and many other countries.

Wherever there is an interest in American literature, the work of F. Scott Fitzgerald has at last "come into its own," and the process is by no means completed. For if a writer like Ernest Hemingway achieved his literary success by eliminating social complexities and "confronting" only those experiences which could be mastered through direct action and ritualized response, one might say that F. Scott Fitzgerald made a success out of "failure" itself. And in the last analysis, we may well wonder which of these two writers has more to tell us of our culture, and our heritage.

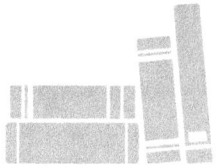

BIBLIOGRAPHY

GENERAL BACKGROUND

Allen, Frederick Lewis. *The Big Change*. New York, 1952.

Cowley, Malcolm. *Exile's Return*. New York, 1961.

Callaghan, Morley. *That Summer in Paris*. New York, 1963.

Hemingway, Ernest. *A Moveable Feast*. New York, 1963.

May, Henry F. *The End of American Innocence*. New York, 1959.

Munson, Gorham. "The Fledgling Years, 1916-1924," *Sewanee Review* XL (1932), 24-34.

Powers, J.F. "Cross Country-St. Paul, Home of the Saints," *Partisan Review* (July, 1949), 714-21.

Wilson, Edmund., ed. *The Crack-Up*. New York, 1945.

CRITICISM AND LITERARY HISTORY

Beach, Joseph Warren. *American Fiction, 1920-1940*. New York, 1941.

Bewley, Marius. *The Eccentric Design*. New York, 1959.

Bishop, John Peale. *Collected Essays of John Peale Bishop*, ed. Edmund Wilson. New York, 1948.

Burgum, Edwin Berry. *The Novel and the World's Dilemma*. New York, 1947.

Chase, Richard. *The Modern Novel and its Tradition*. New York, 1952.

Daiches, David. *The Novel and the Modern World*. New York, 1940.

Fiedler, Leslie. *Love and Death in the American Novel*. Cleveland, 1962.

Geismar, Maxwell. *The Last of the Provincials*. Boston, 1947.

Hoffman, Frederick J. *The Twenties: American Writing In the Postwar Decade*. New York, 1955.

Kazin, Alfred. *On Native Grounds*. New York, 1942.

Millgate, Michael. *American Social Fiction: James to Cozzens*. New York, 1964.

Mizener, Arthur. *The Sense of Life in the Modern Novel*. Boston, 1964.

Muller, Herbert J. *Modern Fiction: A Study in Values*. New York, 1937.

Savage, D. S. *The Withered Branch: Six Studies in the Modern Novel*. London, 1950.

Snell, George. *The Shapers of American Fiction*. New York, 1947.

Thorp, Willard. *American Writing in the Twentieth Century*. Cambridge, 1960.

Wagenknecht, Edward. *Cavalcade of the American Novel*. New York, 1952.

STUDIES AND CRITICAL ANTHOLOGIES ON F. SCOTT FITZGERALD

Eble, Kenneth E. *F. Scott Fitzgerald*. New York, 1963.

Goldhurst, William. *F. Scott Fitzgerald and his Contemporaries*. Cleveland, 1963.

Kazin, Alfred, ed. *F. Scott Fitzgerald: The Man and his Work*. New York, 1962. (a critical anthology).

Miller, James E. *The Fictional Technique of F. Scott Fitzgerald*. The Hague, 1957.

Mizener, Arthur. *The Far Side of Paradise*. Boston, 1951.

Turnbull, Andrew. *F. Scott Fitzgerald*. New York, 1962.

PERIODICAL ESSAYS AND ARTICLES

For an excellent check list of Fitzgerald criticism see the Spring, 1961 issue of *Modern Fiction Studies*. The attention of the student is drawn to the fact that articles in periodicals are an extremely useful and perhaps major source of Fitzgerald criticism. The check list in *Modern Fiction Studies*, and the collection of critical articles noted above (edited by Mizener and Kazin) are very useful secondary reading. Additional suggestions follow:

Barrett, William. "Fitzgerald and America," *Partisan Review* XVIII (May-June, 1951), 345-353.

Bedingfield, Dolores. "Fitzgerald's Corruptible Dream," *Dalhousie Review* XLI (Winter, 1961-62), 513-521.

Bicknell, John W. "The Wasteland of F. Scott Fitzgerald," *Virginia Quarterly Review* XXX (Autumn, 1954), 556-572.

Cardwell, Guy A. "The Lyric World of F. Scott Fitzgerald," *Virginia Quarterly Review* XXXVIII (Spring, 1962), 162-167.

Freidrich, Otto. "F. Scott Fitzgerald: Money, Money, Money," *American Scholar* XXIX (Summer, 1960), 392-405.

Frohock, W.M. "Morals, Manners, and Scott Fitzgerald," *Southwest Review* 40 (Summer, 1955), 220-228.

Fussell, Edwin. "Fitzgerald's Brave New World," *English Literary History* XIX (December, 1952), 291-306.

Hauserman, H.W. "Fitzgerald's Religious Sense," *Modern Fiction Studies* II (Winter, 1956), 81-82.

Jacobsen, Dan. "F. Scott Fitzgerald," *Encounter* XIV (June, 1960), 71-77.

Lubell, Albert J. "The Fitzgerald Revival," *South Atlantic Quarterly* LIV (January, 1955), 95-106.

Mizener, Arthur. "Scott Fitzgerald and the Imaginative Possession of American Life," *Sewanee Review* LIV (Winter, 1946), 66-86.

_____ "Scott Fitzgerald and the 'Top Girl'," *Atlantic Monthly* CCVII (March, 1961), 56.

Troy, William. "The Authority of Failure," *Accent* VI (Autumn, 1945), 56-60.

www.ingramcontent.com/pod-product-compliance
Lightning Source LLC
LaVergne TN
LVHW011738060526
838200LV00051B/3232